AI and the News Industry

Challenges and Opportunities for Journalism

Table of Contents

Chapter 1. Introduction

In the rapidly evolving world of media, the advent of Artificial Intelligence (AI) presents both novel challenges and exciting opportunities. Our special report delves into these fascinating dynamics, shedding light on AI's transformative role in the news industry - from content automation to user personalization, fact-checking, and much more. This report is expertly constructed to appeal to both technophiles and novices alike, explaining complex concepts in a digestible and relatable manner. Whether you're a seasoned journalist, a media mogul, or a curious observer, this comprehensive exploration of AI in journalism will equip you with invaluable insights about the symbiotic relationship between AI and the news. Buy this special report today, and join us on this thrilling journey into the future of journalism.

Chapter 2. The Dawn of AI Journalism

Artificial intelligence (AI) is becoming increasingly ubiquitous across numerous sectors, and journalism is no exception. Modern-day news organizations are increasingly leveraging AI's capabilities to deliver better, faster, and more personalized content. As we begin our exploration of AI in journalism, we first journey back to examine the dawn of this cutting-edge shift in the news industry.

2.1. The Genesis of AI in Journalism

Historically, journalism has adapted to technological advancements, from the printing press to radio, television, and eventually, digital media. AI's increasingly integral role in journalism extends this timeline, adding an additional dimension to the narrative. AI's permeation into journalism has its roots in the early 2010s with programmers exploring ways to automate routine news reporting, particularly in numbers-heavy areas such as business, sports, and elections. Companies like Automated Insights and Narrative Science pioneered this trend, developing AI tools capable of converting raw data into readable news stories.

2.2. The Arrival of Automated News

Automated or AI-generated news content, also known as 'robot journalism,' was among the earliest applications of AI in journalism. Initially, these AI-driven programs could only produce straightforward reports with structured data input. Gradually, they expanded their abilities, producing complex narratives in seconds — a task which would have taken a human journalist significant time and effort. Despite concerns about AI's potential invasion into an essentially human-driven profession, the benefits of speed, accuracy, and the ability to curate massive data quickly rose to prominence.

2.3. Enhancing Accuracy and Speed

The use of AI in journalism ushered in a new era of speed and accuracy. Quakebot, utilized by the Los Angeles Times, exemplified this early adoption of AI for speedy news reporting. Developed as an algorithm, it quickly creates news reports of California earthquakes sourced directly from geological data. The Associated Press similarly employed AI to automate its corporate earnings reports, enabling quicker, wider, and more accurate coverage.

2.4. Personalization and Customization

In the digital age, consumers' expectations of news content have fundamentally shifted. They now demand news that is relevant, timely, and personalized. AI algorithms have taken strides to cater to such personalized needs by curating and recommending news based on user's preferences, reading habits, and browsing history. By extending the passive viewer's active engagement, AI plays a substantial role in redefining the consumption patterns of news audiences.

2.5. Fact-Checking with AI

With misinformation spreading rapidly in today's connected world, fact-checking became essential to maintain the credibility of news outlets. AI tools can crawl millions of articles and social media posts within moments, verifying facts swiftly. While still not as refined as a human journalists' discerning eyes and critical analysis abilities, these tools proved beneficial in minimizing the time and effort committed to fact-checking.

2.6. Downsides and Concerns

Despite the growing adoption and apparent benefits of AI in journalism, its introduction was not without trepidation. Concerns about job security, loss of human touch, algorithmic bias, and accuracy margins were among the early challenges facing the integration of AI in journalism. The risk of propagating misinformation or disinformation inadvertently due to an error in algorithms or misuse by malicious actors has also been a significant concern.

2.7. The State of AI Journalism Today

Over the past decade, AI has steadily gained traction in journalism. As AI technologies become more sophisticated, their support has progressed from simple data-based report creation to enhancing investigation, audience engagement, and making sense of complex narratives. Despite the apprehensions and challenges, AI has profoundly shaped journalism, aiding newsrooms to evolve with the times and address contemporary needs while striving for a balanced fusion of human expertise and machine efficiency.

In the decade since the dawn of AI journalism, the field has evolved symbiotically with advancements in AI technology. From automation to personalization and fact-checking, AI has introduced innovative tools to journalism that have aimed to enhance accuracy, speed, customization, and despite initial fears, job optimization rather than replacement. However, to ensure AI's potential is fully harnessed and its challenges appropriately mitigated, the continuous exploration and regulation of AI in journalism remain vital.

As we close the chapter on AI's genesis in journalism, it is essential to recognize that we are still in the Novus ordo seclorum - the new order of the ages. The capabilities of AI in this field continue to expand, pointing to a future where AI's role in journalism will continue to rise, bearing witness to a narrative that goes beyond the rudimentary interaction of automation and personalization to far-reaching implications on democratization of information, audience engagement, and nuanced storytelling.

Chapter 3. Understanding Algorithms: The Mechanics Behind AI

Deeply woven into the fabric of artificial intelligence (AI) are the complex mathematical and logical processes known as algorithms. It's these very algorithms that allow AI systems to transform raw data into profound insights, make strategic decisions, and deliver unprecedented levels of automation and personalization.

3.1. Algorithms: A Primer

To unpack the mechanics of AI, it's first essential to grasp the basic understanding of what algorithms are. In simple terms, algorithms are sets of step-by-step instructions that guide digital systems in completing a task or solving a problem. They draw upon methodologies from mathematics and logic, structuring data, decision-making processes, and more.

Just as recipes direct the process of baking a cake - combining ingredients in a certain order to achieve a final product - algorithms direct computational processes. However, unlike baking instructions, algorithms must be meticulously designed to handle a myriad array of scenarios, including unforeseen circumstances, and adapt accordingly.

3.2. AI Algorithms: From Decision Trees to Neural Networks

AI algorithms go beyond simple step-by-step procedures. They incorporate advanced techniques to enable machines to learn -

evolve, adapt and improve with exposure to more data. Here some of the widely-used AI algorithms:

1. Decision Trees: Here, decisions are made by traversing 'branches' of 'nodes' representing choices until a final 'leaf' or decision is reached.

2. Regression Algorithms: These are used to predict continuous values by analyzing the relationship between variables.

3. Cluster Algorithms: These are unsupervised algorithms that group similar data points together.

4. Neural Networks: Inspired by biological brains, they work on layers of interconnected 'neurons' to model complex patterns.

Each algorithm serves different needs and is chosen based on the problem at hand, available data, and desired outcomes.

3.3. How Algorithms Propel AI

Underlying any AI system's capacity to learn is the concept of machine learning (ML) algorithms. They are designed to improve with experience, refining their decision-making skills by processing and learning from vast amounts of data.

This 'learning' can take several forms. In supervised learning, the algorithm is presented with input-output pairs, and it learns to predict the output from given inputs. In contrast, unsupervised learning lacks output guidance, forcing the algorithm to find patterns and structures in the provided data.

Then there's reinforcement learning, where an algorithm learns to perform a task by interacting with an environment and receiving rewards or penalties based on its actions.

A striking development in this space is deep learning, a subset of machine learning. Deep learning algorithms - specifically neural networks with numerous layers (deep neural networks) have opened up unparalleled possibilities for AI, particularly in the realm of image and speech recognition.

3.4. Challenges and Opportunities

While the capabilities of AI algorithms are powerful, it's worth noting the challenges involved. The quality of data, the complexity of models, potential biases in data or algorithms, and explainability of AI decisions are all significant concerns.

AI algorithms today are improving at an astonishing rate, fueled by an ever-increasing amount of data and advancements in computing power and storage. The subsequent opportunities such intelligent algorithms can provide to industries - including the news industry - are monumental.

In the realm of news and journalism, algorithms can drive automation and personalization, enabling real-time content curation based on users' preferences and behavior. They can assist in fact-checking, identifying fake news, and highlighting inconsistencies.

However, with these new opportunities also comes an increased responsibility to ensure the use of algorithms aligns with the ethical principles of fairness, accuracy, and transparency.

Understanding AI, and more pertinently, the algorithms that drive it, is a journey of continual learning and discovery. As AI continues to evolve, these algorithms will indubitably continue to shape the way we consume and understand news, pushing the boundaries of journalism in the digital age.

Chapter 4. Automating Journalism: How Bots Write the News

Today's journalism landscape is changing rapidly, and nowhere is this shift more palpable than in the ascendance of automated journalism. Automated journalism, also known as robot journalism, involves the use of AI and algorithms to transform raw data into news stories. In contrast to the traditional model of news production, wherein humans play a central role, the new model often sees bots taking point.

4.1. The Mechanics of Automated Journalism

Automated journalism is based on using structured data - that is, data that is organized in an established model or schema which can be effectively analyzed by an algorithm. Once the data is collected, it is transferred into a software platform. Here, the algorithm, which is designed to transform data into meaningful text, sifts through the data content, isolates the crucial points, and uses a set of pre-programmed rules to structure a news story.

Natural Language Generation (NLG) technology is vital to this process. By enabling computers to write in human language, NLG technology allows news stories to be produced at an unprecedented scale and speed. The articles written by these bots are often indistinguishable from those written by human journalists. They are capable of following grammatical rules, maintaining coherence, and even incorporating a level of storytelling nuance.

4.2. Benefits of Automated Journalism

Automated journalism brings several benefits to the news industry. Once properly set up, the system can generate a large volume of news stories at a fast pace, far exceeding the output of human journalists. It is particularly effective in generating reports on finance, sports, and weather, as these subjects often have readily available structured data.

In addition, automated journalism allows news organizations to cover events that were previously underreported due to resource constraints. This technology enhances objectivity by eliminating the potential for personal bias and is cost-effective, leading to a significant reduction in human resource expenses over time. The speed of content production also keeps pace with the relentless 24/7 news cycle, offering instantaneous reporting capability.

4.3. Challenges and Ethical Questions

Despite its benefits, the advent of automated journalism also introduces novel challenges. The most significant of these concerns is job displacement. As the algorithms become more proficient, there is a rising fear among journalists that AI might replace them. Besides, stories derived from automated journalism are factual and objective but lack the individual perspective, investigative depth, and emotional nuance a human reporter can add to a piece.

Moreover, the ethical implications of automated journalism are a topic of considerable debate among scholars and industry practitioners. Questions around transparency, accountability, and data privacy prevail. If a news organization uses bots to write stories, should it disclose this fact to its readers? Who is responsible when an algorithmic error leads to misinformation?

4.4. Areas of Application and Future Potential

Early adopters of automated journalism, like the Associated Press and Reuters, primarily use algorithms for writing financial earnings reports. Sports journalism is another field ripe for automation, with services like Wordsmith and Automated Insights offering bot-written recaps of games.

Looking forward, pundits predict that AI will be tasked with the role of providing basic reporting, which will free human journalists to focus on interpretative, investigatory, and narrative journalism. Far from making human reporters redundant, AI might invigorate the profession, sparking a journalism renaissance where in-depth, quality reporting is the norm rather than the exception.

4.5. Conclusion

From being a speculative concept, automated journalism has morphed into reality, representing a significant technological leap in the news industry. Its promise of faster and more extensive coverage is intriguing, but ethical quandaries and job displacement fears temper the enthusiasm.

Above all, AI's role in journalism represents the beginning of a profound dialogue about the relationship between technology and human labor, the nature of journalism, and the essence of information in our society. As we further delve into this brave new world of automated journalism, stakeholders must aim for a balance: leveraging the potential of AI while upholding the journalistic values of truth, accuracy, and impartiality. As the lines blur between man and bot, the media industry sits at the cusp of a revolution that is as exciting as it is daunting. Throughout this transformative phase, it is important to remember that while AI is a powerful tool, it is ultimately a means to an end, not an end in itself.

Chapter 5. Personalizing News Experience: AI's user-centric approach

Advancements in technology shift the game in news delivery. Among the key driving forces is Artificial Intelligence - a game-changing phenomenon that is reshaping how news consumers get personalized content. AI adapts to users' preferences, streamlining news to fit each person's expectations and needs. Taking from a panoply of elements comprising user location, content interaction, browsing history, and demographics, AI constructs a customized news journey that truly resonates with the user. Gone are the days of generic newsfeed.

5.1. How AI Personalizes News

A personal news experience commences with the understanding of an end-user's preferences. At the center of this is AI, which utilizes intricate algorithms to analyze and compile users' behavior, interests, and habits. This data, when churned through machine learning models, patterns emerge that help predict future interests, serving information rich, personalized news.

One commonly employed model is the collaborative filtering recommendation system. The online behavior of a user is compared to others, and the AI suggests stories that like-minded users are reading. This provides opportunities for users to discover unexplored interests.

Moreover, content-based filtering focuses on the attributes of items and gives you recommendations based on the similarity between them. For instance, if a user likes a story about an emerging technology, this system would recommend other articles related to that technology.

AI transcends well beyond the simple tracking of users' reading behaviors. Natural language processing (NLP) allows AI systems to understand articles just as humans would. By comprehending the content of articles, AI provides an even richer tailoring of news content.

5.2. Feedback Loop: A Key To Progress

A key component of the personalized news ecosystem is the feedback loop generated by users. Using reinforcement learning, AI finetunes its prediction and selection capabilities based on user engagement with the personalized content. Positive engagement is a signal to deliver more of the same, while negative engagement instructs AI to adjust its offerings. This closed-loop feedback system ensures that the AI continues to learn from users for even better personalization.

5.3. The Rise of News Aggregator Apps

The advent of AI has given rise to personalized news aggregator apps, like Flipboard and Google News. These platforms aggregate news from different sources, delivering customized feeds to users based on their preferences and behavior. The effective use of AI algorithms for content curation and delivery has made such apps increasingly significant in today's news consumption landscape.

Furthermore, mobile push notifications, a product of AI personalization, alert users about news stories as per their preferences. This proactive system keeps users abreast of their areas of interest without their needing to search for these stories.

5.4. Balancing Customization and Information Diversity

While news personalization is an exciting innovation, it poses a potential challenge - that of limiting users to an echo chamber of content. Here, AI must tread a precarious balance, ensuring that users receive news they care about while also presenting diverse viewpoints.

To maintain this balance, some AI systems adopt an 'exploration' strategy, occasionally injecting pieces outside the user's current interests. This approach cushions users from cognitive stagnation while enriching their news experience.

5.5. Defending User Privacy

Personalized news relies heavily on user data. Whilst AI improves user experience, it is essential to have protective measures in place to maintain user privacy. Encrypted algorithms and anonymous data collection strategies can aid in safeguarding information while still capturing useful data. Distributed AI models like federated learning also show promising potential, training the AI on device data without compromising privacy.

5.6. In Summary

Artificial Intelligence is reshaping the way we consume news. By facilitating a user-centric approach, AI can deliver a personalized news experience that matches individual interests and preferences. However, careful measures must be taken to defend user privacy and ensure a diverse information diet. As we continue to explore the capabilities of AI in news personalization, more robust and tailored user journeys will surface.

Chapter 6. The Fact-Checkers: AI in the War against Fake News

In the digital age, fact-checking is more crucial than ever before. Rampant misinformation, propaganda, and the phenomenon known as 'Fake News' pose potent threats to journalism and society at large. AI plays a key role in mitigating these issues. By harnessing Machine Learning (ML) algorithms to parse through information faster and more accurately than humans possibly could, AI fact-checking tools have emerged as a robust line of defense.

6.1. Incorporating AI into Fact-Checking

The first step in combating misinformation is understanding the term 'Fake News.' Misinformation can take many forms: fabricated stories, manipulated images, disinformation campaigns, biased articles, and more. AI can parse through the ambiguities by incorporating Natural Language Processing (NLP) techniques.

NLP researchers successfully trained models to identify indicators of false information, such as sensationalist language, cognitive discrepancies, credibility evaluation, and cross-verification of sources. Once these patterns are identified, they're used to train models to dissect media content, allowing the AI to highlight potential areas of concern.

AI fact-checking potentially addresses two issues: the impossibly broad expanse of information on the Internet and the vast speed at which information spreads. ML algorithms can analyze vast datasets in a fraction of a human's time, making them powerful allies in the fight against misinformation.

6.2. The Role of Deep Learning in Detecting False Information

Deep learning, a subset of ML, performs an even more profound analysis. ML algorithms use numerical and categorical variables, while deep learning uses a process similar to human cognition. It understands the nuances of texts, images, videos, and even audio files—crucial for detecting deep fakes created with cutting-edge technology.

Deep learning models achieve a high degree of accuracy by using artificial neural networks that learn and solve complex problems by mimicking the human brain's structure and function. They are trained to recognize patterns, including those that indicate fake content.

6.3. Challenges in AI Fact-Checking

Despite its vast potential, AI fact-checking is not without challenges. One significant hurdle is the complexity of language and truth. Many false narratives contain grains of truth, making it difficult for AI to discern facts from falsehoods without thorough contextual understanding.

Algorithm bias is another concern. If the dataset used to train the AI is biased, AI will replicate this bias in its judgments. Overcoming this requires data fairness, transparency in making the AI tools, and algorithm accountability.

AI is also susceptible to adversarial attacks where adversaries manipulate input data to mislead AI systems. While AI should not be considered the panacea for misinformation, these utilities have a significant place in our toolkit for combating 'Fake News.'

6.4. Existing Fact-Checkers and Their Impact

Prominent examples of AI-driven fact-checking tools include Full Fact's Live, the Washington Post's Fact Checker, and Factmata. These initiatives leverage AI's abilities to crawl through countless online resources, identify questionable claims, and inspect them vigorously.

While the effectiveness of these fact-checking tools attracts debate, their fundamental value resides in alerting the public about potential misinformation and establishing a culture of transparency and accountability.

6.5. The Potential Future of AI in Fact-Checking

In the future, AI could be used to develop real-time fact-checking systems. Combining deep learning with voice recognition could allow AI systems to fact-check speeches and debates as they occur.

Moreover, AI could assist in debunking misinformation at the source, such as social media platforms, stopping false narratives before they go viral.

Despite the hurdles and unresolved issues that need to be addressed, the potential for AI to revolutionize how we regard truth in media is both an exciting and necessary pursuit. AI's active role in fact-checking has already begun invigorating the fight against 'Fake News.' However, we must recognize its limitations and not become over-reliant on it.

Human discernment remains paramount, and a successful approach will be a hybrid one—combining the tireless efficiency of AI and the nuanced understanding of human fact-checkers. Only by leveraging both can we hope to tip the odds against the proliferation of misinformation and reclaim truth in our digital era.

Chapter 7. Challenges in AI Journalism: Ethics and Credibility

The journalistic landscape continues to be reshaped by the integration of AI-driven technologies. These technological advances not only introduce convenient methods for news compilation and production, but also pose substantial challenges concerning journalistic ethics and credibility. Our assessment presents an in-depth look into these critical issues and provides a framework for addressing ethical dilemmas and credibility considerations in AI journalism.

7.1. Ethical Challenges

AI journalism makes use of automated content production and distribution, altering aspects of journalistic practice traditionally managed by humans. The resulting implications bring about numerous ethical dilemmas.

One significant ethical challenge revolves around accountability. With AI being a central player in gathering and disseminating posts, it might be unclear who is accountable when a story causes harm. This unsettlement emerges due to the shared responsibility between the AI algorithms, human editors, and the AI developers, leading to an ethical quandary which we currently lack comprehensive solutions for.

Bias in AI is another profound ethical concern. AI systems rely on patterns in training data to make decisions. Consequently, any bias present in the training data, whether relating to gender, race, or socio-economic status, can inadvertently be replicated and perpetuated by the AI system. This introduces prejudice and inequity into the foundational layers of AI journalism.

Moreover, AI-driven journalism is entirely dependent on data and access to information. Consequently, it raises critical questions about privacy. For efficient news generation, AI has to gather substantial amounts of information, creating potential risks for privacy infringement.

Striking the right balance between efficiency and ethical obligations is thus a cornerstone challenge in AI journalism.

7.2. Credibility Challenges

The credibility of news is sophisticatedly tied to its accuracy, impartiality, and objectivity. However, introducing AI into the mix can jeopardize all these qualities, concomitantly impacting the overall credibility.

The accuracy of data is one integral component of news credibility. An error in data input can lead to skewed news reports, disinformation, and misinformation. Since AI systems are reliant on the quality of the input data, the risk of inaccuracy amplifies. Furthermore, the incapability of AI in discerning nuances and contextual values in news further exacerbates this.

Impartiality gets compromised when AI systems reproduce and fortify existing biases as mentioned earlier. However, it also takes a hit when algorithms personalize news delivery based on user preferences - an increasingly common practice in the digital age. This leads to further polarization of views and an "echo chamber" effect, significantly tarnishing impartiality and fostering biases.

Furthermore, the process of AI news generation lacks transparency. Most AI systems functioning today are based on complex neural networks, often referred to as "black boxes" due to their opaqueness. This obscure process affects journalists' understanding of their reporting, hampering the intentionality that supports objectivity.

7.3. Addressing the Challenges

Considering the ramifications of these challenges, it is crucial to generate feasible solutions.

Transparency and accountability can mitigate many of the stated problems. Openness about the AI's role in news generation and clear guidelines about accountability responsibility can help establish credibility. Transparency also encourages public trust and helps evaluate the impartiality and objectivity of news stories.

To combat biases, more inclusive and diverse training data could be utilized. Rigorous testing and refining of algorithms to identify and mitigate potential biases can help.

Privacy concerns can be alleviated by establishing robust policies on data collection, use, and storage. Consent-based data collection, anonymization of personal data, strict regulatory compliance are some pivotal steps towards ensuring privacy.

Despite the complexities these issues present, ethical and credibility challenges in AI journalism are not insurmountable. With deliberate and vigilant measures, we can adopt productive methods that substantially undercut the associated risks, harnessing the full potential of AI in the journalism sector.

Chapter 8. The Machine Learning Revolution: Optimizing News Production

The transformation of news production in the current era is underpinned by the advent of machine learning (ML) - a field of artificial intelligence that empowers computers to learn from data and consequently to enhance their performance without human intervention. Machine learning is being utilized to automate and optimize news production processes, from content generation, editing, and packaging, to distribution and reception.

8.1. Machine Learning: A Primer

Before jumping into its applications, it is essential to understand the basic principles of machine learning. Machine learning, at its core, involves the development of algorithms enabling computers to learn independently from data – that is, to enhance their performance or decision-making capabilities in a given task without being explicitly programmed to do so.

Machine learning can be roughly divided into two main types: supervised and unsupervised. Supervised learning involves training a model on a labeled dataset to predict outcomes or classify new unlabeled data. In contrast, unsupervised learning involves discovering patterns and relationships in unlabeled datasets without any predefined categories or outcomes, good examples of which are clustering and association.

8.2. Automating Content Generation

One of the primary applications of machine learning in news

production is in automating content generation. News organizations employ Natural Language Generation (NLG) algorithms, a subfield of AI, to generate news stories from structured data. These stories are usually fact-based and don't require a high level of nuanced analysis, such as financial earnings reports, sports scores, and weather forecasts.

The Associated Press (AP), for example, uses an NLG system to transform raw financial data into narratives. In another instance, the LA Times uses a robot reporter called "Quakebot" that pulls seismic data from the US Geological Survey to automatically write and publish articles about earthquakes.

Machine learning also assists in producing news summaries and extracts. Algorithms are used to extract key points from lengthy articles or reports, helping in the publication of snippets for mobile platforms or audio briefings for smart speakers – essential formats in an increasingly digital and mobile-first world.

8.3. Optimizing Editing and Packaging

Traditional news editing involves tasks such as fact-checking, detecting bias, ensuring clarity and consistency, and much more. Machine learning can assist human editors by automating some of these tasks, thus streamlining the news packaging process.

Fact-checking, in particular, can be automated to an extent using machine learning. Algorithms can be trained to cross-verify details in a news story with a database of verified facts. Automated systems can also be tailored to detect bias or polarized language, helping editors make the final product as neutral and objective as possible.

Another facet of news production where machine learning is making strides is video editing. Machine learning algorithms can be trained to categorize, tag, and annotate video content. This automated process can aid in quickly locating key segments or identifying sentiment, aiding in the creation of compelling video packages and reducing manual labor.

8.4. Personalizing News Delivery

The advent of digital news platforms led to an overwhelming abundance of content available to consumers. Machine learning provides a way out of this information overload through personalization.

By understanding an individual's reading habits, interests, and behavior, machine learning can create dynamic, personalized news feeds for individual readers. It's not just about what kind of stories a reader might enjoy; it's also about when they're likely to want them.

Moreover, machine learning can also personalize the mode of news delivery. Based on usage patterns, the system can determine whether a user prefers text articles, audio summaries, video content, or visual infographics and deliver the news in the preferred format.

8.5. Potential Challenges and Ethical Considerations

While machine learning promises to revolutionize news production, it does not come devoid of challenges and ethical considerations. However, the most significant challenge hinges on the risk of bias in machine learning algorithms. Since these algorithms are trained on existing data, they can inadvertently perpetuate existing biases present in the training data. This issue calls for critical scrutiny in how the training data is curated.

Moreover, the increasing automation of news production processes also raises questions about job security for journalists and editors. It calls for a necessary shift in the role of journalists from mere reporters to data analysts, news curators, and content strategists.

Machine learning might also lead to an increased dependence on third-party technology providers, potentially affecting the independence of news organizations. Issues of transparency, accountability, and user privacy also need to be navigated carefully in this new found automation.

The future of news production is exciting, and machine learning is undeniably at the forefront. However, the road to this future should be paved with thoughtful considerations to ensure that the integrity and purpose of journalism are preserved and enhanced.

In the end, machine learning is a powerful tool. Leveraged judiciously, it has the potential to reinvent the landscape of news production, delivering faster, more accurate, personalized, and globally accessible news to audiences worldwide.

Chapter 9. Impact on Employment: AI and the Journalism Workforce

Newsrooms worldwide grapple with narratives about Artificial Intelligence inevitably phasing humanworkers out. These narratives paint a pervasive picture of AI being a harbinger of joblessness, poised to make numerous roles within the journalism workforce redundant. However, this overview also provides an opportune moment to examine the potential of AI in enhancing, rather than replacing, human capital within the industry. This chapter will explore the impact of AI on employment in journalism through the prism of disruption, collaboration, and revolution.

9.1. Disruption: Redefining Roles and Tasks within Journalism

The integration of AI into the news industry is disrupting established daily routines, positional hierarchies, and established workflows. It is transforming mundane, manual tasks into automated processes, freeing journalists to focus on tasks that require human intelligence.

An AI subfield known as Natural Language Generation (NLG) can process and interpret structured data to create narratives indistinguishable from human-authored content. AP News, for instance, uses AI to produce thousands of financial earning report articles each quarter, a task formerly done by its reporters. This approach has allowed journalists to dig deep into analytical roles, producing stories with more profound contexts.

As AI automates low-level tasks, journalists are moving to more complex endeavours like investigative journalism and critical analysis. It is an essential disruption, reframing roles within the newsroom and allowing journalists to leverage their unique skills, like their ability to engage with sources, probe, and contextualize stories.

9.2. Collaboration: Humans and Machines Working Together

The advent of AI in newsrooms is not a zero-sum game where machines will entirely supersede human journalists. Instead, it offers a scenario of collaboration where machines and humans coexist, each performing tasks most suited to their abilities, and supplementing each other's work.

The Washington Post's Heliograf is a quintessential example of this collaboration. In the 2016 US elections, Heliograf produced short updates about the election results, allowing the newspaper's human journalists to focus on analysing the implications of those results or other crucial tasks.

Such technology can prove to be indispensable in large-scale journalistic investigations. The Panama Papers, one of the most significant data leaks in journalistic history, required sifting through millions of documents – an enormous task made manageable by AI-enabled document mining tools. Without these tools, human journalists would have been overwhelmed.

In such scenarios, the categorizations of tasks based on their suitability for AI or humans become clear. AI tackles the number-crunching, data analysis, and basic story generation, while humans will thrive in areas requiring emotional intelligence, cultural understanding, and ethical judgement.

9.3. Revolution: Creation of New Job Roles

Far from only causing displacement, the integration of AI into journalism is paving the way for entirely new roles within the industry. News organizations including The New York Times, Quartz, and ProPublica have hired editors tasked with leading their AI and automation efforts, creating positions like machine learning editors and bot developers.

However, creating these roles is more than just introducing new job titles – it involves rethinking journalism curricula to incorporate AI training and data science. This evolution isn't just within the scope of large organizations. Smaller, local newsrooms should assess how they could benefit from AI while lobbying for needed resources and training. By doing so, they can ensure their workforces remain relevant in an age of growing automation.

The incorporation of AI also necessitates a new range of ethical codes and guidelines to be formulated within newsrooms. The training of AI systems and the checking of their output will involve journalists, data scientists, and ethical officers, thereby creating a multidisciplinary blend of skills.

Despite concerns about job loss due to AI's pervasive integration into the news industry, evidence suggests that AI will add value to journalists' roles instead of removing them. The collaboration of AI and journalists can lead to improved news coverage, the automation of mundane tasks, and the creation of new job roles within the journalism industry. This AI-led revolution isn't just altering the landscape of journalism but is shaping up to deliver an industry that is sharper, more streamlined, and effective. Recognizing this potential and adapting accordingly will be crucial to journalism's future, and that of its workforce. AI's impact on journalism employment should not be viewed as a threat but rather as a catalyst for change and progress.

Chapter 10. How AI is Shaping the Business of News

In the landscape of contemporary journalism, the integration and advancement of Artificial Intelligence (AI) is finding more substantial footing with each passing day. While this phenomenon has brought forth a plethora of lucrative opportunities, it also ushers in an era of challenges that are just as invigorating. Herein, we delve into the ways AI operates as the modern-day game changer for the business of news, while also considering the potential barriers to its integration.

10.1. The Automation Revelation

From the generation of financial reports to dissemination of weather updates, AI, through automation, is eroding the significance of manual content creation. News providers leverage technologies such as Natural Language Generation (NLG) and Machine Learning (ML) to simplify the process of news production, thereby increasing efficiency and reducing errors.

Rapid advancements in AI have facilitated the development of algorithms capable of interpreting available data to produce news articles. This development has been particularly useful in finance and sports journalism where numerical data is abundant.

An automatic content generation has massive economic implications. Using AI technology to create articles or reports instead of manually compiling them dramatically decreases production costs. As such, news providers can use their budget more effectively, putting resources into hiring skilled analysts and reporters who can intervene where AI might not suffice.

10.2. Personalization: The New norm

The news industry is not solely about news production; it is equally about catering to the varied interests of readers. AI-mediated personalization has risen to prominence for news providers to establish a stronger rapport with their audience. Personalized content not only enhances the user experience but also aids in customer retention by presenting users with articles that align with their specific interests.

Algorithms also enable the monitoring of individual's reading history and preferences, thereby creating personalized news feeds. For example, Google News employs AI to create a 'For You' section comprising stories based on the user's previous search histories and interactions.

10.3. Reimagining Advertising

In a digital world where user attention is a valuable commodity, AI is revolutionizing advertising, a critical revenue source for news businesses. AI's precision-targeting capability ensures that advertising becomes more efficient, less intrusive, and closely aligned with user interests.

By processing user data, AI can predict user preferences allowing for the placement of tailored ads. Thus, adverts are far more likely to be clicked on and purchased from, maximizing ad revenues for the news outlets.

10.4. Fighting Fake News: Creation of Trust

Despite the monumental strides made in AI-driven news production, a recurring menace - the spread of misinformation or fake news - threatens the credibility of the journalism industry. To stifle this concern, AI acts as the primary line of defense.

Automated algorithms, such as Deep Learning models, help identify discrepancies and inconsistencies in news articles by comparing them with a massive archive of verified content. They can detect counterfeit images, discern harmful content, and identify deepfakes - hyper-realistic forged video or audio material. In doing so, these algorithms elevate the standards of fact-checking, fostering trustworthy journalism.

This rigorous fact-checking capability of AI can curate a healthier information environment by debunking falsities and unsubstantiated rumors quickly. Thus, it builds a formidable rapport with readers, thereby promoting authenticity.

10.5. Challenges and Ethical Considerations

Alongside the tremendous potential, questions and challenges about the use of AI in the news industry persist. Privacy issues arise from the personal data used for personalized news feeds and targeted advertising. There are ethical considerations concerning the replacement of journalists by AI algorithms for content generation.

The transparency of these algorithms is essential too. Currently, we are primarily dealing with 'black-box' AI, which means that users and even creators cannot discern how the algorithms reach decisions. This issue poses serious problems for a sector like journalism, where ethical decision-making is paramount.

Artificial Intelligence's integration into journalism signifies the dawn of a promising, yet challenging era. The prospects of automation, personalization, and fact-checking capabilities of AI herald an era of efficiency and veracity in the news industry. Conversely, associated challenges, mainly ethical and privacy concerns, prompt a broader conversation about AI governance in journalism and, indeed, the digital space at large.

In this journey towards AI integration, news businesses, tech giants, policymakers, and society must make conscientious strides, collectively. Careful execution alongside rigorous regulation can equip AI to revolutionize not just the business of news, but also the very essence of journalism - its credibility, transparency, and duty towards societal enlightenment.

Chapter 11. Looking Ahead: The Future of AI in News Media

In the not too distant past, media professionals orated compelling narratives to the public. Today, we're transitioning into an era where AI generates and delivers news reports, creating an unprecedented shift within the news industry. The subsequent unfolding of events will undoubtedly have profound implications for journalists, the recipient audience, and society in general.

AI is not merely a high-speed, robotic copywriter; it has the potential to reshape how news is gathered, processed, written, edited, and distributed. But what does the future of AI in news media actually look like? Let's explore.

11.1. USING AI FOR NEWS GENERATION AND AUTOMATION

One area AI has proven excellent is report automation. AI can convert structured data into readable text rapidly, covering specialized fields that require routine updates and instant reportage like sports scores, stock reports, and weather updates. These automated articles have unprecedented speed and scale, while also maintaining accuracy – an invaluable asset in 24-hour news domains.

Organizations like Associated Press and Bloomberg have already incorporated Automated Insights and Cyborg, AI writing tools that can generate thousands of articles per second. Others, like the Washington Post, have developed homegrown tools, such as Heliograf.

What's interesting is the evolution of these tools to handle unstructured data, news blogging, and original report writing. The day when AI surpasses repetition and reportage to bring depth and perspective to news articles isn't too far away.

11.2. AI IN NEWS PERSONALIZATION

A universal truth of content is that it must cater to its audience. However, in the world of news, comprehending readers' preferences and customizing content accordingly is no small feat. This is another area where AI shines.

Traditionally, website cookies and registration data served as the primary means of customizing news. Today, AI can analyze reading histories or habits to create personalized news recommendations. Machine learning algorithms can predict a reader's interests with incredible precision, pushing relevant articles to their feed and in turn fostering reader loyalty.

The BBC and The New York Times already utilize such algorithms to deliver customized content to readers. Looking forward, experts believe that AI can even consider a reader's mood or context for further personalization.

11.3. AI IN STREAMLINING NEWSROOM OPERATIONS

Beyond front-facing functions, AI will reform newsroom operations and editorial workflows. Predictive intelligence can help in assigning reporters to cover stories, optimizing news schedules, or predicting potential influence of released articles.

Moreover, algorithms can monitor content runtime and suggest necessary modifications for optimum engagement. It will allow journalists to focus on storytelling and investigation, leaving routine tasks to AI.

11.4. AI IN FACT-CHECKING AND FIGHTING FAKE NEWS

As the 24-hour news cycle provides a perpetual information flow, the need for fact-checking has never been more crucial. AI can streamline this process and help detect and flag fake news.

Initiatives like Full Fact in the UK and Chequeado in Argentina are employing AI for real-time fact checking. They use AI to scan the internet and check the presented facts against a vast database of credible sources.

AI can even spot deepfakes, arguably the most dangerous form of fake news which involves the manipulation of video and audio to create believable, but entirely false content. This could be a game-changer in our fight against disseminating fraudulent information.

11.5. AI IN OFFERING AUGMENTED JOURNALISM

In the future, AI will also assist journalists in their investigation. By sifting through public data or running number crunching processes, AI can unearth potential story ideas and angles that avoid human bias or oversight.

AI has the potential to democratize journalism by giving smaller organizations access to these investigative resources. This could result in an environment of diverse narratives with balanced reportage.

11.6. CONCLUSION: CHALLENGES AND OPPORTUNITIES

The era of AI in journalism bristles with challenges and opportunities. Concerns regarding AI bias, data privacy, and job security of journalists are valid and warrant discussion.

However, the potential benefits – increased reportage, personalized delivery, improved operational efficiency, advanced fact-checking, and augmented journalism – advocate for embracing AI. It's essential for the news industry to engage in a pragmatic conversation about AI, aiming for a pivotal balance between embracing its potential and addressing its challenges.

Tomorrow's newsroom will undoubtedly encompass AI technologies; it's only a question of 'how' rather than 'if.' The challenge for the news industry is to direct the AI narrative towards the creation of quality journalism that upholds ethical standards and serves the public good. After all, AI is a tool and, like any tool, its value lies in how we use it.

With thoughtfulness, foresight, and constructive dialogue among technologists, journalists, policy-makers, and the public, we can shape an exciting future for AI in news media, one where technology is not a rival but a companion in the pursuit of delivering quality news.